WING
Gooftun

Blackfield Junior School
Hampton Lane
Blackfield
Southampton SO4 1XA

*For my three grandchildren,
Elizabeth and Sophia Bennetts,
and Matthew Macowan.*

Written by Marlene J. Bennetts
Illustrated by Julie McCormack

© 1995 Shortland Publications Inc.

03 02 01 00 99 98
11 10 9 8 7 6 5 4 3

All rights reserved.

Published by Shortland Publications Inc.
Produced by Shortland Publications,
2B Cawley Street, Ellerslie, Auckland, New Zealand
Distributed in Australia by Rigby Heinemann,
a division of Reed International Books Australia Pty Ltd.
ACN 001 002 357, 22 Salmon Street, Port Melbourne, Victoria 3207
Distributed in the United Kingdom by Kingscourt Publishing Limited,
P.O. Box 1427, Freepost, London W6 9BR

Printed through Bookbuilders Limited, Hong Kong.

ISBN: 0-7901-0993-X

CONTENTS

Chapter 1	5
Chapter 2	14
Chapter 3	20
Chapter 4	27
Chapter 5	36
Chapter 6	41
Chapter 7	46
Chapter 8	57
Chapter 9	61

CHAPTER 1

The shrill sound of scraping claws sliding down the iron roof of the house woke her with a start. It looked like the keas were up to their early morning tricks again.

When the young keas first arrived at their cabin a couple of days ago, her father said, "Now, Anna, make sure you don't feed them – it's absolutely against park rules."

"I know, Dad. Uncle Jeff told me how the keas get lazy if they're hand fed, and how they won't go into the forest to search for berries and larvae."

"Besides, Anna, understand that they're pretty inquisitive birds, and are apt to get into trouble if they stay too long in the township. So don't feed them, OK?"

At first, she didn't feed the olive-green parrots. Instead, she was content to watch them perform their comical displays. How she laughed when they swung and rolled over the branches. It was as if they were performing a special acrobatic show just for her.

The keas amused the tourists, too – especially when they tried to peck at the camera lenses and the people's heavy woollen socks. Sometimes, though, the tourists got pretty annoyed with the birds. They weren't quite as charming when they ripped the leather handles off backpacks, shredded coats with their strong beaks, and ripped off the rubber seals from parked cars.

Despite all that, Anna still loved them. The five keas that particularly interested her wore different-coloured rings on their legs. The Conservation Department banded all the keas in the national park, so they could record the native parrots' ages, and when they died.

The largest of the keas wore a red leg band and was the group's leader. It pushed in front of the other four keas and strutted around like a soldier on parade. At the same time, it fixed its black eyes on her as if to say, "I hope you're paying attention – watch this!" Then, off it flew to a tree branch, where it rolled and tumbled over and over until it was dizzy. The large green bird looked so goofy that Anna quickly decided to name it "Gooftah."

At the end of the performance, Gooftah perched on the branch and stared at Anna with an expression that clearly showed he was waiting for his well-deserved reward.

"One slice of bread couldn't harm the keas, could it?" she thought. And that first slice of bread was immediately gobbled up.

As the days passed, she found herself feeding the keas more and more slices of bread. At first, the keas still left the township to gather more food in the bush. But lately, since she'd been feeding them so much and so often, they were never far from her back door.

She knew she was going to have to stop feeding them soon, or else her parents and Uncle Jeff would notice that the keas had become permanent house guests.

❊❊✹❊❊

Anna and her family had travelled to New Zealand from Canada to visit her adored Uncle Jeff – her mother's youngest brother, who was a national park ranger. They were to be "Down Under" for a whole month, and Uncle Jeff had done everything he could to ensure their trip would be spectacular.

It was turning out to be that and more, especially for Anna. In the few weeks she'd been there, Anna had accompanied her Uncle Jeff and Aunt Susan on camping trips to check out the distant bush tracks and huts. They'd made other exciting excursions to repair swing bridges damaged by rain-swollen rivers.

Aunt Susan, who grew up in the New Zealand bush, was practically a ranger herself. She wasn't scared of walking across the wobbly swing bridges that hung high above rushing rivers. And she never complained about the thousands of biting sandflies, either.

Even the day-to-day work was fun, from cleaning up after a storm to replenishing the piles of firewood stacked by the hut doors. In this past month, Anna had decided to become a park ranger herself. It was all she could think about. That's why she didn't want to disappoint any of her family by letting them find out that she had broken the rules – especially her uncle and aunt, who had done so much to make sure she'd have a good time.

※※✳︎※※

Biting off a yawn, she sat up quickly in bed. Today, she was going to take care of the kea problem once and for all. She hopped out of bed and walked over to the window. Pulling the curtains aside, she leaned out and looked for the keas.

"Good morning, Gooftah," she said, seeing the large kea strutting across the grass nearby. "You think you're going to get some breakfast, don't you?" she chuckled.

Gooftah came closer to the house, cocked his head on one side, and gave her a wink.

Anna leaned further out the window and whispered, "Well, forget it! Today is the day you guys become wild keas again. Shoo! Go away, Gooftah! You and your buddies need to get back to the bush. Scram!"

With a high-pitched, indignant "keeaw", Gooftah flew away, showing off his scarlet underwings, and joined his friends on the roof of a nearby cabin.

Anna turned her gaze to the snow-capped mountains rimming the valley. Blankets of fog hung on the densely wooded foothills, draping the small settlement. Puffs of mist swirled low over the train station down the road from their cabin.

With the arrival of colder weather, the tourist season was shutting down, and all but two of the cabins around the small park settlement were deserted. Although the scenery was beautiful, and Anna could normally have looked at it for hours, today it made her kind of sad. She knew that her own holidays would soon be ending, too.

With a shiver, Anna closed the window against the chilly breeze, and turned to get dressed for the day. When she entered the kitchen, she overheard her parents talking.

"Those ridiculous keas woke me up at dawn," complained Anna's mother. "I can't understand why they're hanging around our cabin all the time."

Anna sat down and started to eat without saying a word.

"Hmmm," her dad mumbled as he enjoyed his toast and marmalade. "You're right, Beth," he said, swallowing the last bite. "I've never heard of them acting that way. I wonder if some of the tourists are feeding them."

"I can't imagine why anyone would do that with all of the "Don't feed the birds" signs around," Mum replied. "All the same, maybe we should keep an eye on them to help Jeff out."

"Daddy," Anna's six-year-old sister piped up, "I know who's feeding them…"

Anna quickly kicked at her under the table.

"OUCH!" Megan yelled, her eyes filling up with tears. "Stop kicking, Anna!"

"Anna!" Her mother looked sternly at her. "Don't tell me *you've* been feeding them – after all we told you!"

Anna hung her head. "Only a few pieces of bread, Mum," she stammered. "I didn't think it would hurt them."

"Now, Anna," her father began, "feeding keas bread is the same as you eating junk food. It's not

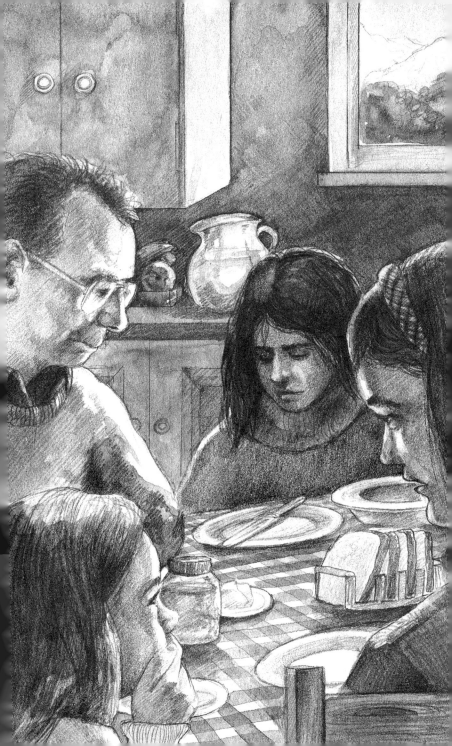

good for them, and it keeps them from eating the food they need. You know better than that! No wonder the keas aren't bothering to go out and hunt!"

"But, Dad, I only gave them a little bit." Anna swallowed hard.

"What's a 'little bit'?"

She pulled her gaze away from his inquisitive hazel eyes. "Well, I gave them a loaf of stale bread. I suppose…" she began, and then changed her mind about trying to come up with a good excuse. "I'm sorry, Mum and Dad. Please don't tell Uncle Jeff, or else he…"

"Or else he won't think you're responsible enough to be a ranger when you grow up, right?" Dad smiled at her in spite of himself. "All right, honey. But please remember that those signs about not feeding the birds apply to you just as much as they do to any visitor here, OK?"

"I understand, Dad. Thanks."

"I *told* you not to feed them, Anna," Megan gloated. "Anna's in trouble… Anna's in trouble…"

"Oh, be quiet, Megan," Anna muttered.

The day had not got off to a good start.

CHAPTER

2

After the disaster at breakfast, Anna couldn't wait to get outside. As she was doing up her hiking boots, Mum called her.

"Anna, could you please look for Megan and see what she's up to."

Anna put down her backpack and went to look for her sister, grumbling as she went. Megan could be a real pain sometimes… Anna often wished that her sister was closer to her own age – *especially* on this trip, when she didn't have any of her own friends around. It would be great to have someone to do things with.

Anna found her sister playing in her room.

"Thanks a lot, Megan," she said. "I didn't appreciate getting into trouble back there. Did you ever think that the keas will probably leave now that no one's feeding them?"

"I – I'm sorry, Anna." Megan's face crumpled, as she, too, had become fond of the funny birds.

Anna just glared at her and, feeling only slightly guilty about being such a bully, turned away to report to her mum.

"Meg's in her room playing, Mum," she called down the hall. "I'm going to go pick up the rubbish for Uncle Jeff." Then, grabbing her backpack, she headed out the door.

✻

As she walked around the settlement, dumping the rubbish into a big bag, she had a lot to think about. Mostly, she hoped that her parents wouldn't tell Uncle Jeff about what she had done.

"A ranger has to keep the park's rules better than anyone else," her uncle often said whenever she mentioned her dream to him. "Remember that those rules are made to protect both the wildlife *and* the people."

Yes, her uncle was great. He never nagged her

to hurry when she couldn't keep up with him on a difficult track. Instead, he'd say he was a little tired or hungry himself, and suggest taking a break.

As she was rounding the loop in sight of the last cabin, with her big rubbish bag bursting full, Anna ran into Mr McNabb, one of the other tourists staying in the cabins.

"So, I see you're collecting the rubbish just like a good little ranger," he said, with a sneer that made the comment seem more of an insult than a compliment.

She nodded, and wondered why in the world he didn't offer to help her carry the huge bag. In fact, that was not the only strange thing about Mr McNabb. He always made her feel uncomfortable. She didn't like the way his thin, black moustache wiggled when he talked, and she really didn't like the way his steely, grey eyes shifted back and forth all the time.

"Just thought I might walk to the lookout to see the keas," he said, slowing down to keep pace with her. "My wife wants to paint them. She's just fascinated by them, so I thought I'd check out the situation for her."

As they arrived in the enclave, Anna saw her dad chopping up wood over by her cabin. Relieved that the walk was over, she smiled briefly at Mr McNabb, and turned her back on him to empty her bag. She couldn't put her finger on it, but something about that man really bothered her. She wondered what his wife was like – nobody had ever seen her at all, even though the couple had been staying there for almost a week.

She turned around and started when she saw that Mr McNabb was still there, leaning against one of the buildings. Why hadn't he gone onto the lookout?

"I thought I saw some keas flying around *your* cabin this morning, Junior Ranger," he drawled quietly, making sure no one else could hear.

Anna just nodded at him.

Mr McNabb kept talking. "The man at the Information Office told me the lookout was the best place to see the keas. He said they spend most of their time up there. If that's true, now why would they be staying down here?"

Anna answered carefully. "Well, I wouldn't

know," she fibbed, not wanting to share too much information. "I hope he also told you not to feed them?"

"Ohhhh, yeah," he said nonchalantly. "Sure he did."

Anna just stared at him, hoping that he would leave. You know, she thought to herself, he doesn't *look* like he's out for a walk. Even though the morning was cold, he wasn't wearing or carrying a heavy coat. And he was wearing dress shoes, not the sturdy boots that were recommended for the track.

"Forgot to change them," Mr McNabb snapped, noticing her glance at his feet. Then he turned and headed back towards his cabin, which lay in the exact opposite direction of the lookout.

Very strange, Anna thought, watching him walk away. Very strange.

CHAPTER 3

"Hmm?" Anna turned to her mum, who had been talking to her. She'd been day-dreaming, watching the snow clouds build up against the mountains. "Sorry, Mum, I wasn't paying attention."

"I said," Mum smiled at her, "that your uncle is getting off work early today so he can join us for dinner."

"Hey, that's great!" Anna answered. "What can I do to help you get ready?"

"Well, you could take Megan out to play for awhile. She's been cooped up in here all afternoon because of the cold weather, and she's getting pretty restless. Why don't you two run this letter over to the McNabbs' – it was left here by mistake."

Anna didn't want to make any more trouble after what had happened at breakfast, so she quietly went to put on her coat and find her sister.

Megan was thrilled to be out with her older sister, and started running around. "I'll race you, Anna!" she shrieked. "I'll race you there!" She ran ahead up the path to the McNabbs' cabin.

Anna followed her slowly, thinking about the McNabbs. She wondered if she should have mentioned anything about their strange behaviour to her Mum… Before she knew it, she was at their cabin.

"I won! I won!" Megan crowed delightedly, dancing around. "I beat Anna!"

"Oh, be quiet, Megan," Anna groaned. "What will the McNabbs think?" Just then, before she could even knock, Mr McNabb swung the door open and poked his long, thin nose out.

"Hey! What are you kids doing hanging around here?" he barked.

"Um, we were just bringing you your mail," Anna stammered. Megan, surprised by his harsh tone, had frozen in her tracks.

He snatched it out of her hands and, without

even thanking them for their trouble, shut the door in their faces. Anna turned and faced her sister, who looked just as shocked as she felt herself. Before either of them could say anything, they heard a loud "Keeaw!" directly above their heads.

There, perched on the edge of the McNabbs' roof, was Gooftah, looking smugly down at them.

"Gooftah, what on earth are you doing up there?" Anna asked him. By now, since she wasn't feeding them, he and his friends should have taken off into the bush to find food. She looked around and saw the rest of the keas sitting further up on the roof. They didn't look hungry. In fact, they were preening their feathers with very self-satisfied expressions on their faces.

Perplexed, she put her hand on her sister's shoulder and was just leading her away when she came up against her father, who was on his way back from a walk. He had a stern expression on his face.

"Anna, what are those birds still doing here? I thought we talked about this already – have you been feeding them?"

"Of course not, Dad," Anna said, feeling hurt. "I told you I wouldn't do it anymore, and I haven't."

"I'm sorry, Anna, I just had to make sure. You did promise, and I do believe you." He smiled down at her. "Hey, let's drop off your sister back at the cabin to help out your mother, and then why don't we run into town together to get some supplies for tonight's dinner?"

Anna grinned back at him and went to wait by the car while Dad told Mum where they were going. While she waited, she was surprised to see that, from the car, she had a great view of the McNabbs' cabin. She was even more surprised when she saw Mr McNabb open up the door and throw out some food – a lot of food – to the birds.

Without thinking, she started down the path to confront him. As she approached, though, she remembered how creepy he was and thought better of it. It would really be a lot smarter to just go back and tell her parents about the whole thing. But it was too late! Mr McNabb had seen her coming, and was now walking up to *her*, with an expression on his face that frightened her. Anna froze.

"Well, now, what's wrong, Junior Ranger?" He flashed her an oily smile. "Are you upset that your kea friends have decided to pay the poor old McNabbs a little visit?"

Anna stood her ground and tried to look brave, even though she wanted to turn and run back to her cabin. She tilted up her chin and met his gaze.

"My wife just wanted those nice birds to stay around for a day or two. It makes it much easier for her to paint if she can do it down here. I think that walk up to the lookout would just be too hard on her, don't you? It's awfully cold, and you can't expect a nice lady like her to go walking around in this kind of weather, now, can you?" he asked. Anna felt he was trying too hard to look friendly – it made her uncomfortable.

"You know it's against the rules," she began coldly. "You and your wife could get into a lot of trouble if you're caught feeding the keas."

"Well, that's very interesting, Junior Ranger," Mr McNabb sneered, losing his greasy smile. "Did *you* get in trouble for feeding them?"

Noting that he had caught Anna completely

off guard, he continued, "I *thought* that was why they were hanging around here in the first place. Now, we're only going to keep them here for another day or two while my wife paints, so we're not causing any *real* harm, now are we? Why don't you just pretend you didn't see us feeding them, and we'll pretend we didn't see you feeding them, and everything will be just fine." He gave her a hard look and, taking her stunned silence as an agreement, turned and slouched back to his cabin.

Anna turned and walked miserably back to the car where her father was now waiting for her. As much as she hated the idea of anyone else finding out that she had fed the birds, she almost hated the idea of keeping a secret for that awful Mr McNabb even more. She just didn't know what to do.

CHAPTER

4

"I'll help your mum with the dishes, Anna," Uncle Jeff said that evening after dinner.

"Why don't you and your sister go and watch one of those videos I brought you guys from town."

Anna, who normally loved anything that got her away from doing dishes, hesitated. She knew that Uncle Jeff wanted to talk to her parents in private about something – she'd heard him say so when he'd arrived – and she was tired of being lumped in with Megan as "too young" whenever anything interesting happened.

"Go on, Anna," her mum said, steering her towards the door. "Why don't you have a night off! Celebrate!"

Megan was looking excitedly through the movies when Anna entered. "What do you want to see, Anna? Look! He even brought us some cartoons!"

Anna, who was trying to overhear the conversation in the kitchen, turned to her impatiently. "Put on whatever you want, Meg. I'll be right back."

She sneaked back down the hall and stood just outside the kitchen door, which was slightly ajar.

"They're fetching about $10,000 each on the overseas black market," Uncle Jeff was saying. "A number of birds have been captured down here in the South Island. Goodness knows how the smugglers are getting them out of New Zealand – those keas can sound like sirens when they're frightened! Our office has been told to watch for anything suspicious, so I thought I'd enlist your help while you're here. We can use the extra eyes and ears."

Kea smugglers! Anna's mind was reeling as she tiptoed back down the hall to join Megan. She was so absorbed in her thoughts that she hardly noticed when the adults joined them awhile later. With a start, she realized Uncle Jeff was speaking to her.

"Anna, Earth calling Anna!" he laughed, "let me try this again. Anna," he said formally, smothering a broad smile, "do you want to come hiking with your Aunt Susan and me this weekend?"

"Of course! That'd be great!" Then, immediately after answering, she lapsed back into deep thought. She couldn't stop thinking about the smugglers. It would be just awful if her keas were captured! Then Anna smiled to herself. She would just have to make sure that they weren't.

※※✳※※

Later that night, as she lay in bed, she tried to think about the problem the way a real detective would. She tried to picture what the smugglers would look like. They'd have shifty eyes. Yes, that's it. Shifty eyes and thin, black moustaches. Just like Mr McNabb.

Anna sat up suddenly. She'd always thought that there was something strange about Mr McNabb. And now, after hearing about the smugglers, she was going to be sure to keep a close watch on him. She lay back in bed, trying to figure out how she could start her investigation.

※※✱※※

The next morning, Anna woke very early to the sound of the keas sliding down the iron roof of her cabin. Relief washed over her – the keas were still safe! During the night she'd had nightmares that they'd been captured, and she couldn't do anything to rescue them.

She looked at her watch. Six o'clock! Boy, it was even earlier than she had thought – no one in her family would be up for at least another hour. It was the perfect time for Anna to begin her detective work. As she threw on her clothes, she thought up a story. I'll go down there, she thought, tugging on her boots, and take their milk to them. That way, if they see me, Mr McNabb will just make another crack about what a conscientious "Junior Ranger" I am. I really don't like that man.

The same thought kept turning over and over in her mind as she ran through the still-dark bush to the McNabbs' cabin. As her eyes adjusted to the dim light, she was able to make out the shapes of the keas on the grass.

Apparently, they had given up on *her* feeding them and gone to the McNabbs'. Anna couldn't decide whether to run up and scare them away, or just hide and watch. Before she could make up her mind, the door to the cabin opened and Mr McNabb and a woman Anna guessed to be his wife poked their heads out. Anna ducked back behind the bushes, not wanting to be seen.

"I don't know why you made me wake up so early, Floyd," the woman yawned. "Those stupid birds could have waited awhile longer."

"Well, Myra," he snapped, "we want to take care of this before anyone notices, and the earlier we finish, the earlier we can get out of this crummy hole in the woods, right!" He turned his back on her abruptly and started flinging chunks of bread at the birds.

The violence of his throws startled the birds, and they shied away from the food. Mr McNabb stifled his impatience, and in his slimiest voice, started coaxing the keas to eat.

"Here you go," he gushed, "nice birds. Eat the special bread Myra made for you."

As the keas drew near, he started to chuckle – a sound that made Anna's blood run cold. She started to shiver, and tried to keep quiet so she wouldn't give herself away. Still, she couldn't help gasping when she saw what happened next.

Gooftah, who had been the first one to eat, stopped in mid gulp, froze, and toppled over on the ground. One by one, the other birds followed. The McNabbs didn't hear Anna, though. They were obviously too thrilled at the sight to pay attention to anything else.

"It worked, Floyd! It worked like a charm!" the woman raved, earning her a scornful glance from her husband.

"Of course it did, Myra, it always has. Now prove that I didn't make a mistake bringing you on this trip by helping me collect these birds!"

Expertly, the McNabbs grabbed the birds and hauled them inside. Hardly waiting for them to shut the door, Anna shot out of her hiding-place and raced back to her cabin. Breathless and terrified, she burst into the kitchen, looking for her parents.

"Mum! Dad! Come quick! Something terrible's happened! Muuuuuum!"

Anna's parents, awoken by her shouts, came rushing down the hall, wrapping their bathrobes around them to keep warm.

"What, Anna, what? Are you OK? Is Megan OK?" Anna's parents ran up to her, panicked.

"Yes! We're fine! It's the keas! They've taken the keas!" Anna was so upset she could hardly get the words out.

"Calm down, Anna," her father said sternly. "What are you talking about? What about keas?"

"They've *TAKEN* them! The smugglers are the McNabbs – they did it! It's just what Uncle Jeff was talking about last night. They did it, they stole our keas!" Anna knew there wasn't a moment to lose. Why were her parents taking so long to understand?

Her mum turned to her dad. "She must have overheard Jeff. I guess it's given her nightmares." Mum turned back to Anna. "Now, Anna, did you have a bad dream? You know, it really isn't a good idea to go around accusing people like that."

"NO!" Anna found herself shouting, and

tried to calm herself so she could convince her parents. "No, it wasn't a dream. The McNabbs have been feeding the keas; and this morning, I saw them give the birds some bread with something on it that knocked out Gooftah and his four friends. Please," she begged, "please, we've got to do something to help them."

Her parents looked at each other, seemed to reach some sort of a silent agreement, and turned back to face her.

"OK, Anna. We believe you about the McNabbs. Now start at the beginning and tell us everything you know."

CHAPTER 5

Why was all this taking so long? Anna was getting very frustrated.

As she spilled out her story, her parents had questioned every little detail surrounding the McNabbs. Now, they were lecturing her about eavesdropping! If they didn't do something soon, the McNabbs would never be caught!

"I'm sorry about eavesdropping, but I did – and I'm glad." Anna was trying to control her impatience, but not succeeding very well. "Now if we don't do something quick, it won't matter! Can't we please call Uncle Jeff?"

"Of course, Anna. We just had to make sure we have enough to go on." Anna's dad smiled at her, pulling his coat on over his pyjamas. "You've done a good job, by the way. Now let's see what we can do. Beth," he said, turning to his wife, "you call Jeff, and I'll run up and see if we can't just stop the McNabbs now." He walked briskly out the door.

Mum started dialling the phone immediately. "Hello, Jeff? Sorry to call so early, but we have a bit of an emergency here." She quickly described the situation; and just as she was finishing, Dad came running back into the kitchen.

"Sure enough," he panted, "they're gone! Looks like Anna was right about them!"

Mum told Uncle Jeff and then hung up the phone. "He's on his way. He's also pretty proud of you, young lady," she said, smiling at Anna.

Anna fidgeted the whole time she was eating breakfast. What if they couldn't stop the McNabbs? What if the birds were taken to a foreign country and sold? She hoped they were OK – that poison couldn't have been too good for them!

When Uncle Jeff arrived, he didn't waste a lot of time questioning Anna. Instead, he just verified a couple of key facts and asked her if there was anything else she could remember.

Anna brightened. There sure was. "Uncle Jeff," she said excitedly, "I know their car's licence plate number! I memorized it when I was on my way down to watch them this morning."

"That's my girl! Now why don't you get your coat and come down to the ranger station with me. You can tell the chief all about it, while I get the search started." He beamed at her.

On the way to the station, Uncle Jeff filled her in on the rest of the details about the smugglers that she hadn't heard the night before. Anna listened, aghast. Apparently, the smugglers normally stole quite a few more birds than they thought they could sell because many of the animals wouldn't survive the trip. She could barely get that thought out of her mind, even when Uncle Jeff introduced her to the chief ranger.

The chief asked her a lot of questions, and she was there, retelling her story for almost a full hour before Uncle Jeff came back into the room.

"Chief, they were in a rental car, and the company says it hasn't been returned yet. I wonder where they're going!"

"Well," the chief ranger said, giving Anna a wink, "let's get going on the job our detective here brought us. I'll contact the police and alert the customs people at the international airport. Jeff, you run Anna home, and then head back here for your briefing. Don't worry, Anna, thanks to your help, I think we'll be able to find those keas."

CHAPTER 6

Anna paced up and down inside the cabin, watching the phone, willing it to ring. Before Uncle Jeff had dropped her off and started searching for the McNabbs, she had made him promise to call her as soon as there were any new developments. But so far, nothing.

Finally during dinner, she couldn't stand it any longer. "Mum, can I please call Uncle Jeff? This waiting is killing me!"

"Now, Anna, your uncle said he would call *you*," Mum said understandingly. She knew Anna was doing her best to be patient.

"He also said that it could be quite a long wait, since they couldn't really do anything until the McNabbs made some sort of a move. Sorry, honey, it looks like we'll just have to sit here and wait."

"I know," Anna groaned. "I just wish I could have gone with them. Maybe I could have done something… *anything*. No matter what, it would have been better than staying here and not knowing!"

By bedtime, Anna had given up hope of hearing anything. She went to bed and couldn't sleep because of all of the thoughts rushing around in her head. She kept picturing all kinds of awful things that could be happening to the keas. Gooftah and his friends are probably in Asia by now, she thought sadly. Finally, after she had decided it was the longest night of her life, she fell into a restless sleep.

Later that night, she woke to the shattering sound of the phone ringing in the darkness. Instantly alert, she sat up in bed, hoping it was Uncle Jeff, but too worried about the keas' fate to go and answer herself. When her father called her to come to the phone, she shot out of bed.

"Hello," she said breathlessly, "Uncle Jeff? Have you found the keas?"

"Well, Anna, thanks to you, we did." Uncle Jeff sounded very tired. "Customs intercepted the McNabbs when they were trying to catch a flight out just a little while ago."

"But the keas! Are they all right?" Anna could hardly bear the suspense.

"One of them died, Anna, and the other four are being cared for by a city vet. I'm sorry we weren't able to save all of them."

Anna shut her eyes. Please let it not be Gooftah, she thought. Then, gulping, she asked, "Did the one who died have a red leg band?"

"I don't know. Customs didn't say."

Anna was still worrying about Gooftah when Uncle Jeff broke in.

"Anna, would you like to come to the city with me tomorrow? I'll be talking to the vet early in the morning, and if the keas are well enough to travel, I'd love to have a little company to bring them home."

"Of course!" Anna's spirits started to climb. Finally she could do something! And soon she'd be able to find out for herself if Gooftah was alive or not.

"Well, get some sleep, and I'll call you tomorrow," Uncle Jeff said before hanging up.

Anna walked back to her bed. Get some sleep, she thought wryly. That wasn't going to be easy. Not with the thoughts she kept having of Gooftah's limp body being carried away by the McNabbs.

CHAPTER 7

When Anna awoke the next morning, she knew that something seemed strange even before she opened her eyes. Of course! She was so used to being woken up by the sound of keas sliding down the roof that the morning didn't seem right without it. In fact, it seemed that she'd slept much later than normal. She looked at her watch. Eight o'clock!

She jumped out of bed and ran down the hall. "Mum! Did Uncle Jeff call? Why didn't you wake me up? He's going to be here soon!"

Her mum smiled at her. "Yes, he called and will be here soon. I was just coming to wake you up to tell you – I thought you could use a little extra sleep after last night's excitement."

Anna ran back down the hall to throw on her clothes. Even though she hurried, Uncle Jeff was waiting by the time she got back to the kitchen.

"Hi! I'm all ready to go," she exclaimed, giving him a big hug.

"No you're not, young lady," her mum retorted. "You need to get some breakfast in you before you head out the door. And that," she said, silencing Anna's protest, "will give your uncle a chance to update us *all* on the news."

Anna sat down impatiently and started shoving food in her mouth. She slowed down only when her uncle assured her that they had plenty of time. He helped himself to a cup of coffee while he told his story.

"Well," he began, "Customs caught the McNabbs when they were checking in at the airport. When they opened their suitcases, the officials found the birds stuffed inside. The keas had been heavily drugged, and were stuffed in cardboard cylinders, like the kind you put posters in." He frowned. "It wasn't a very humane way to treat them – that's why one of them suffocated. I'm kind of surprised that more of them didn't."

"I hope the McNabbs get the punishment they deserve," Anna's dad broke in indignantly.

"It looks like they could end up in prison," Uncle Jeff replied. "I'm pretty sure from Anna's story that this isn't their first offence. At the very least, they're going to get hit with a heavy fine and will lose their passports. By the way," he added, "I got a message from the vet this morning, and she said the other birds are doing fine, and we can bring them home today."

"Did she say whether one of them had a red leg band?" Anna asked hopefully.

"No, she didn't, Anna, but we'll soon be able to see for ourselves. Are you ready?"

※※✳※※

Later, as they drove along the road leading to the city, Anna gazed out at the snow-covered mountains. Normally she would have been thrilled by the dazzling sun shining on the breathtaking white mountains and the purple foothills nestled below; but today, all she could think about was seeing her keas again.

"Please let Gooftah be alive," she thought over and over, as the long drive led them into the outskirts of the city.

"We're nearly there, Anna – you can probably stop pushing the car," Uncle Jeff chuckled.

Anna laughed herself, releasing some of the tension when she realized that her feet were pushing hard against the floorboards, as if she was trying to help the car go faster.

Just minutes later, they pulled up to a long, low, white building. Springing out of the car, Anna ran ahead, too excited to wait for her uncle. She rocked back and forth from one foot to the other while they waited for the vet to appear. Finally, they entered the room that held the keas. While her uncle spoke with the vet, Anna hurriedly peered into cage after cage, looking for Gooftah.

In the first cage, a single small kea rested. It wasn't big enough to be Gooftah.

In the second cage, another two keas were preening themselves. Anna checked the colour of the leg bands. Yellow and blue. No Gooftah!

Holding her breath, Anna approached the third cage. There was a large parrot huddled

inside, feathers ruffled out so that she couldn't see the leg band.

"Gooftah," she breathed, "Gooftah, is it you?"

The parrot stretched its wings and moved cautiously towards her. There it was! She caught a glimpse of red on his leg.

"It *is* you! You're OK!" She spun around to Uncle Jeff. "Oh, he's OK! I'm so glad!"

The vet broke into her happiness. "That big

one there really scared me. Much longer in that tube, and I can't say that he would have made it. They were all in pretty bad shape from the drugs, as it was. Lack of air didn't do much to help, either."

Her voice sounded angry, Anna thought. She was glad that the keas had been brought to someone who cared so much. She turned and was gazing back into the cage when she heard the vet say something else that sent her heart into her throat.

"Actually, I'd prefer it if you could give me another couple of hours with that big one there," she was saying. "I'm really not completely happy with his progress, and I'd like to see him eat some food before his long trip home."

What? Gooftah not eating? He was always the hungriest of the bunch! Anna started to worry again.

"Do you think he'll get better?" she asked, with a tremor in her voice.

Uncle Jeff put his hand on her shoulder. "Of course he will, Anna," he said reassuringly. "Let's just give the vet a chance to work with him a little more, and we can run some errands while we wait. How about if I take you out for some lunch to celebrate your successful detective work?"

Anna reluctantly agreed and followed him out to the car. She tried as hard as she could to listen to his light chatter.

And later, when he took her to a toy store to pick out a present for Megan, she had a hard time remembering the kinds of toys her little sister liked.

※※✱※※

At last it was time to return to the vet's.

"Now, Anna, I'm counting on you to take care of this bird on his trip back home," the vet said, a twinkle in her eye lightening the seriousness in her voice. "I think you might be just the person to make sure he gets there intact."

Anna nodded. Gooftah still hadn't eaten anything, and he didn't look his usual lively self, but the vet had given them permission to take the birds home.

She'd said that it was possible that Gooftah just wasn't comfortable enough in the strange surroundings to take care of himself.

Anna helped load the birds into the car and watched them carefully while Uncle Jeff drove. The whole time, she kept wishing she knew what to do to get Gooftah to eat.

When they were almost home, she tentatively suggested to Uncle Jeff that maybe they should give Gooftah some bread.

"Now, Anna," Uncle Jeff said, knitting his brows, "what would make you think that a kea would like bread. You wouldn't have any personal experience in the matter, would you?"

"Oh, Uncle Jeff, who told you?" Anna was terribly embarrassed. "It was Megan, wasn't it? Of course it was – who else? I'm so sorry. I knew it was wrong, and I'd even stopped doing it…" Her voice trailed off miserably. Uncle Jeff was never going to trust her again!

"Well, let's just say a little bird told me," he answered, with his exaggerated frown. Anna peeked over at him and saw that he was trying not to smile. "Anna, I won't lecture you about it. I think the past couple of days have probably taught you enough of a lesson. Let's just say, this was maybe your first and biggest lesson about being a ranger. You always have to follow the rules – even more than anyone else does."

What? Uncle Jeff still thought that she could grow up and be a ranger. What a relief! Yes, she thought silently, it was a lesson she'd never forget!

"Now, about your suggestion of feeding the keas some bread…" Uncle Jeff said a few moments later. "I've been thinking about it and, while it seems kind and could help them get stronger immediately, the most humane thing to do in the long run is to just leave them alone. They need to *unlearn* the fact that they can get food from humans so that they can survive on their own."

So saying, he pulled up to the mountain lookout and shut off the engine. "Now how about a hand in setting these poor birds free, hmm?"

Anna and her uncle unloaded the cages and opened the doors. The keas, which had been growing increasingly restless on the trip back, scurried out and started stretching their wings. At least, three of them did. Gooftah, the big, bold parrot, hung back dejectedly on the cage floor.

"Come on, Gooftah," Anna said softly. "You're home, and you're safe." She put in her hand and softly scooped the bird out onto the grass. "What's wrong with him, Uncle Jeff?" she asked worriedly.

"Maybe he just needs a moment," Uncle Jeff guessed. "Let's give him some time."

As he spoke, the big bird started to look around, and Anna could almost see his interest start to pick up. Eventually he took a short flight up to a nearby branch.

"Come on, Gooftah!" Anna cried, "Fly!"

"Anna, down here we say 'wing high' – it means fly freely," Uncle Jeff said softly; and at the words, the big bird lifted up and flew off without looking back.

"Wing high, Gooftah," Anna repeated under her breath. "Oh, please take care, and wing high."

CHAPTER

8

Anna's eyes burned in her head, exhausted from staring into the bush. This was the third day she'd spent up at the lookout, hoping to glimpse Gooftah. There was still no sign of him anywhere. What if he hadn't started eating? What if he was still sick from being drugged? The weather was so cold – maybe he wasn't going to make it.

She dragged herself back down the hill to the cabin. She knew her mother would be getting impatient about packing. They were going home the next day and, so far, Anna hadn't even started getting organized.

When she stepped into the cabin, her parents and Megan were waiting for her.

"Anna," her father began, a strange note

sounding in his deep voice, "we just got a call from the chief ranger. He wants to see you this evening. Why don't you clean up and then we can get going."

Anna looked up, startled. "What... Why? I don't understand. Do you think he found out I fed the keas?" Her stomach started to churn.

"Well, Anna, you'll just have to wait and speak to him, now, won't you?" her mother said.

"Anna... I know a se-cr..." Megan began in a singsong voice, but her mother playfully clapped a hand over her mouth. She tried to finish her sentence, but stopped under her father's stern look.

In a daze, Anna changed clothes and climbed into the car with her family. What are they going to do to me, she wondered. I really didn't mean any harm, and I *did* learn my lesson.

"Come on, Anna," her dad encouraged when she lagged behind, not wanting to go into the ranger station. "Don't worry, we're here to lend you moral support, and we'll make sure they don't tighten the thumbscrews too much!"

"Stop!" Mum elbowed Dad in the ribs. "You're scaring her to death!"

Anna gulped and went up to the chief's desk. "You wanted to see me, sir?" she stammered.

"Yes, I do, young lady," the chief said in a deep voice. "Could you please turn and face that camera over there?"

Anna glanced over at the large television camera that she'd been too worried to notice on her way into the room. She just shook her head, unable to understand what was happening to her.

The chief ranger gave her a crisp salute. "Anna," he began, "the Conservation Department is very grateful for your help in catching the kea smugglers. They've asked me to present you with this Junior Conservation award as a sign of our appreciation." The chief's face split into a kind smile as he handed Anna the trophy and certificate.

Anna couldn't believe what was happening. Surely this was a sign that one day she would make a good park ranger after all!

CHAPTER 9

It was time to go. Still, Anna had to hurry back to the lookout one more time – she just had to take a final look for Gooftah before she left. She couldn't bear the thought of not knowing what had happened to her favourite bird.

"AAA-NNNA!" Oh no, there was her dad. It was time to go. She scanned the surroundings one last time.

She saw several keas, but not the large one with the red-banded leg. No, he wasn't there. She would never know if he was OK.

She ran down the path, fighting back tears. When she reached the cabin, she blindly reached for her backpack that was waiting by the door, the only thing left to be stowed in the car.

She was just walking reluctantly to the car when… above her rang out a loud, raucous, glorious noise. "Keeaw!"

There he was! There was Gooftah, hanging upside down from the iron roof of the cabin, flapping his large wings and looking as wonderfully alive as he ever had.

Anna gasped. He was OK! She turned to look at him, knowing that she had only a moment to say goodbye. It seemed to her that as she did so, he winked at her.

"Wing high, Gooftah!" she yelled up at him triumphantly, and the bird burst into flight – his strong, green body flashing with red as he soared above her. "Wing high!"

TITLES IN THE SERIES

SET 9A

Television Drama
Time for Sale
The Shady Deal
The Loch Ness Monster Mystery
Secrets of the Desert

SET 9B

To JJ From CC
Pandora's Box
The Birthday Disaster
The Song of the Mantis
Helping the Hoiho

SET 9C

Glumly
Rupert and the Griffin
The Tree, the Trunk, and the Tuba
Errol the Peril
Cassidy's Magic

SET 9D

Barney
Get a Grip, Pip!
Casey's Case
Dear Future
Strange Meetings

SET 10A

A Battle of Words
The Rainbow Solution
Fortune's Friend
Eureka
It's a Frog's Life

SET 10B

The Cat Burglar of Pethaven Drive
The Matchbox
In Search of the Great Bears
Many Happy Returns
Spider Relatives

SET 10C

Horrible Hank
Brian's Brilliant Career
Fernitickles
It's All in Your Mind,
  James Robert
Wing High, Gooftah

SET 10D

The Week of the Jellyhoppers
Timothy Whuffenpuffen-
  Whippersnapper
Timedetectors
Ryan's Dog Ringo
The Secret of Kiribu Tapu Lagoon